LIVING JEWISH VALUES

Family Connections

Mark H. Levine

BEHRMAN HOUSE

Behrman House, Inc.

www.behrmanhouse.com

In memory of my beloved parents, Arnold and Martha Levine, who built a home filled with harmony, appreciation, truth, and holiness.

Mark H. Levine

Design: **Jill A. Winitzer, WinitzerDesign.com**

The publisher gratefully acknowledges the following sources of photographs:
Cover Yuri Arcurs/Shutterstock; **ii** Noam Armonn/Shutterstock; **2** iQoncept/Shutterstock; **6** Wikimedia Commons; **7** Walter Green, Hay House Publishing; **8, 24** Antonio Abrignani/Shutterstock; **9** Joint/Shutterstock; **11, 21, 31, 41** Lena Sergeeva/Shutterstock, Oksvik/Shutterstock; **12** Yuri Arcurs/Shutterstock; **18** mementoil/istock; **19** Sigrid Estrada; **20** helza/Shutterstock; **22** Andy Dean Photography/Shutterstock; **25** Innocence Project; **36** Athos Boncompagni Illustratore/Shutterstock; **37** Wikimedia Commons

CONTENTS

INTRODUCTION

Fire swept through the Holy Temple, consuming everything in its voracious path. Roman troops, who had besieged Jerusalem for months, finally breached the city's walls and utterly destroyed God's dwelling place on earth.

During the next two hundred years, the rabbinic sages of our tradition rebuilt the Jewish religion. Instead of the old system of priests and sacrifices, they established prayer and the performance of good deeds as pathways to God. Rather than centralizing worship in one sacred spot, they decided that each Jewish home should be a *mikdash m'at*, a miniature sanctuary. Family life, therefore, became the focal point of Judaism. As a result, many of our most important religious rituals take place with our families in our homes.

This book, Family Connections, is volume two in the Living Jewish Values series. In it, you will explore four Jewish values that strengthen family relationships:

Hakarat Hatov – Gratitude
Sh'lom Bayit – Family Harmony
Emet – Truth
Kedushah – Holiness

Teaching you about these values is the task of this book. Hopefully, the legends, personality quizzes, role model profiles, concept maps, and journal activities will make the learning enjoyable. Adopting the values, however, is your responsibility. Trying out new behaviors can be challenging, but the task is not beyond your reach. As you begin, you might find inspiration from Moses's final words of encouragement to the children of Israel:

"Surely, this Instruction which I enjoin upon you this day is not too baffling for you, nor is it beyond your reach. It is not in the heavens, that you should say, 'Who among us can go up to the heavens and get it for us and impart it to us, that we may observe it? …'No, the thing is very close to you, in your mouth and in your heart, to observe it." *(Deuteronomy 30:11–14)*

CHAPTER 1

Hakarat Hatov

Rabbi Simeon ben Halafta panted heavily as he and his daughter trudged home from the market in the blazing midday heat. When his stubby legs could not carry his obese body one step farther, the rabbi collapsed on the ground. "Fan me with your fan," he asked his daughter, "and I will reward you with a jar of precious spikenard oil." But before the girl could obey, a cool breeze blew in from the sea, reviving her father. "How many jars of spikenard oil do I owe the owner of that breeze?" said Rabbi Simeon. (*Baba Metzia 86a*)

Gratitude

The Jewish value הַכָּרַת הַטוֹב (*hakarat hatov*), which literally means "recognizing the good," should be easy to practice. After all, when good things happen, they are readily apparent—for example, a friend helps us study for a test, or our parents pay for us to go to camp, or a dutiful daughter fans her exhausted father. At moments like these, we recognize our good fortune and feel grateful to those who have extended goodness to us. When we acknowledge the goodness and say thank you, we demonstrate respect for the giver.

But the fullest measure of *hakarat hatov*, of sincere gratitude, involves expressing thanks not only for the obvious goodness we experience from those around us, but also for the goodnesses of daily life that we too often overlook, such as waking up in the morning, eating fresh fruit at breakfast, or feeling a soothing breeze on a hot day. Judaism encourages us to thank God, the Creator of all, for daily miracles like these. When we acknowledge God's presence in all things great and small, we cultivate a sense of wonder for the world, and a sense of humility in our place in it.

CULTIVATE GRATITUDE — BE HAPPY

Scientists are discovering that an attitude of gratitude has many benefits, including:

- LOWER levels of stress
- GREATER well-being
- BETTER attitudes about school and family relations
- BETTER health
- FASTER progress on achieving personal and academic goals

ACTIVITY 1

Developing an attitude of gratitude involves changing your perspective. Instead of focusing on what you do not have, shift your attention to all the gifts you enjoy. In the gratitude glasses below, list strategies that will help you shift your attention.
The examples will help you get started.

Gratitude Strengthens My Family
Keep a family gratitude list on the refrigerator

_____

_____

_____

_____

Gratitude Enriches My Friendships
Write anonymous notes of gratitude and hide them where your friends will find them

_____

_____

_____

_____

What Position Do You Play?

When others are generous to you, how do you show your appreciation?
Take this quiz and find out!

After a friend helps you study for a hard test, you would most likely:

◆ Offer to help her study for the next subject she struggles with.

◆ Find the friend and tell her, "Thanks."

◆ Run and show your parents your good grade.

When you receive a compliment after a really tough day, you:

◆ Graciously accept it and tell the person that the compliment lifted your spirits.

◆ Return the compliment by admiring the other person's shirt or shoes.

◆ Wonder why only one person complimented you that day.

The first time your parents let you go alone to the mall with friends, you:

◆ Thanked them for recognizing how mature and responsible you are.

◆ Jumped up and down, and ran through the house screaming in victory.

◆ Cleaned up your room without being asked.

When you get over a nasty cold, you:

◆ Breathe a sigh of relief that you won't miss any more after-school activities.

◆ Decide to wash your hands more often.

◆ Thank God for your good health and clear sinuses.

When your parents give you money for the movies, you most likely:

◆ Text your friends to rave about the show.

◆ Offer to do an extra chore when you get home.

◆ Send a text message of thanks to them immediately after the show.

Mostly blue
Punter in football
You're a special teams member, and you show appreciation only on special occasions. Think about expressing your gratitude more frequently. As Hillel teaches, "If I am only for myself, what am I?" *(Pirkei Avot 1:14).*

Mostly green
Left field in softball
You're always on the field, but you don't always see action. Likewise, you are regularly appreciative, but choose to express your gratitude in deeds rather than words. As the Mishnah says, "Say little and do much" *(Pirkei Avot 1:15).*

Mostly red
Point guard in basketball
Your position is always in play. You're the quickest player on the team, and the quickest person to say thank you to others for what they do for you. As the Midrash teaches, "With every single breath we take, we must express our gratitude to God" *(Genesis Rabbah 14:9).*

AGADDIC TRADITION

"It wasn't my fault," Leah cried to her maidservant, "and yet Jacob treats me as if I were responsible for deceiving him on his wedding night. Even now, after giving him three beautiful sons, I'm certain he hates me."

Leah rubbed her eyes, which were red and swollen from crying. "It's silly to think that this child I'm now carrying inside me will change things," she said, her voice trailing off softly.

Zilpah nodded in agreement but said nothing. Her mind, though, raced with kind and empathic thoughts that she had felt for her mistress for years. *How has she lived with such self-doubt?* she wondered. *What did it feel like to have been scorned by Jacob in favor of Rachel? How could she regain her self-esteem after hearing Jacob scream at her father, "What is this that you have done to me?"* when Jacob realized he had married Leah instead of Rachel?

"I feel so alone," Leah sobbed. Her anguished cry brought Zilpah back to the present, and the maidservant moved quickly to the pregnant woman's side.

"You love me, don't you, Zilpah?"

"Yes, Leah. And God loves you; after all, the Creator has blessed you with three sons—and soon your fourth child will enter the world."

The baby was born that day. When Leah saw the newborn infant, she cast aside her sorrow and exclaimed, "This time I will thank God." In gratitude to God, Leah named the baby boy Judah (*Yehudah*), which means "Thanks to God."

ACTIVITY 2

1. Why do you think Leah was able to set aside her sorrow and expess gratitude when the baby was born? _____

_____

2. The Jewish people are called *Yehudim*, a noun derived from Judah's name, *Yehudah*. This connection highlights the importance of gratitude in the Jewish religion. How do Jews demonstrate gratitude?

_____

_____

3. Our religious sages have taught that gratitude cannot coexist with arrogance or selfishness. Why not?

_____

_____

HAKARAT HATOV SUPERSTAR

For fifty years the two men had shared a close friendship, but like many men of their generation, they kept their deepest feelings to themselves. Now, the older man lay dying in a hospital. When the younger man heard the news, he traveled across the country to be at his friend's bedside.

For five days they sat together and swapped stories of their past. But each day ended without an acknowledgement of how much they meant to each other. When the last day of the visit arrived, both men realized that the younger man would leave and they would never see each other again.

Suddenly, the dying man struggled to get up. Thinking that something was wrong, the younger man leapt to his feet. He was ready to race to the nursing station. The older man stepped forward with his arms open wide. The men hugged tightly in an embrace that was fifty years overdue.

"I love you," said the younger man.

"I know," replied his friend.

When he returned home, the younger man wrote a gratitude letter to his lifelong friend. He described what their friendship meant to him and how much he appreciated the older man. As he read the letter, the older man cried, and then he called his friend to assure him that he too was grateful for all they had shared.

FOREWORD BY KEN BLANCHARD
#1 *New York Times* best-selling author

THIS IS THE
MOMENT!

How One Man's Yearlong Journey Captured
the Power of Extraordinary Gratitude

WALTER GREEN

The emotional encounter between these two friends was inspired by Walter Green, and he describes it in his book *This Is the Moment*. Green's book recounts the year he devoted to expressing his sincere gratitude to friends and family who influenced his life. "Even though I'd always placed a high value on my own relationships," writes Green, "I'd never specifically articulated to these individuals what each of them meant to me."

Hakarat Hatov

Biblical Era

First Fruit Offering at the Temple

The obligation to offer the first fruits of the harvest in gratitude to God is described in the Book of Deuteronomy. After a joyous processional into Jerusalem, each person would place their basket of offerings before God at the Temple and recite:

"My ancestors were wandering Arameans. They went down to Egypt with meager numbers and there became a great and populous nation. The Egyptians dealt harshly with us and oppressed us; they imposed heavy labor upon us. We cried to Adonai, the God of our ancestors, and God heard our plea and saw our plight, our misery, and our oppression. God freed us from Egypt by a mighty hand, by an outstretched arm and awesome power, and by signs and portents. God brought us to this place and gave us this land."

1. Underline the expression(s) of gratitude in this recitation.

2. Why does the oath recount the events of the Exodus from Egypt?

Thanksgiving Sacrifice at the Temple

Voluntary sacrifice in gratitude for God's bounty but obligatory after escaping a life-threatening crisis.

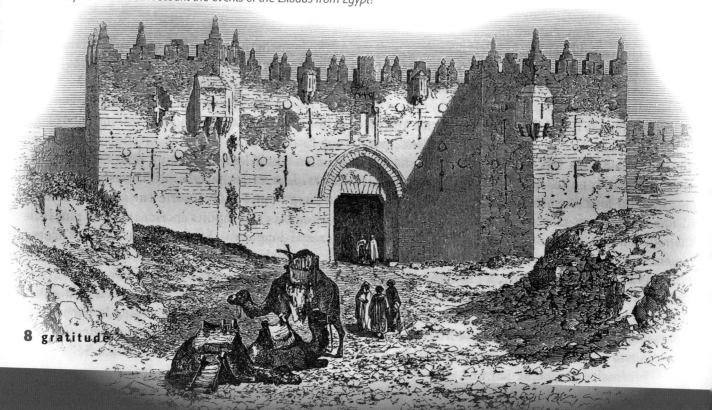

CONCEPT MAP

Rabbinic Era

After the Temple was destroyed, sacrifices were replaced by prayers. Our sages developed blessings for us to say whenever we experience God's goodness, including seeing magnificent natural beauty. The thanksgiving sacrifice for escaping a life-threatening crisis also became a prayer, called *Birkat Hagomel.*

The Talmud prescribes that the following people should offer gratitude to God:

1. Those who have completed sea voyages
2. Those who have arrived at settlements after passing through the desert
3. Those who have recovered from an illness
4. Those who have been freed from prison

"Blessed are You, Adonai, our God, Ruler of the universe, who bestows kindness on those who are committed, and who has granted to me all kindness." The congregation responds: "May the One who has granted you all kindness always grant kindness to you."

Modern Era

We recite *Birkat Hagomel* as our ancestors did, but we include additional opportunities to express our gratitude.

Today, it's appropriate to recite *Birkat Hagomel* when God delivers us from any danger, physical or emotional.

Our Creative Expressions of Gratitude

Each generation of Jews adds their own prayers of gratitude to God.

Use this space to write an original blessing or poem acknowledging God's goodness in the world.

_____

_____

_____

_____

_____

_____

_____

ACTIVITY 3

Adopting *hakarat hatov* as part of our lives takes practice.

Write a gratitude for each topic mentioned in the calendar below.

Here are three tips to writing a meaningful gratitude:

BE SPECIFIC

TELL WHY YOU'RE GRATEFUL

EXPLAIN WHY IT'S IMPORTANT TO YOU

5 Sunday	6 Monday	7 Tuesday	8 Wednesday	9 Thursday	10 Erev Shabbat	11 Shabbat
Parents	A sibling	Close relatives	Favorite teacher	Best friends	My neighborhood	My school
12 Sunday	13 Monday	14 Tuesday	15 Wednesday	16 Thursday	17 Erev Shabbat	18 Shabbat
Music	Winter	Nature	U.S. government	Israel	A hero	God

WHAT I THINK

When we recognize the good that others do for us, our thankfulness is a sign of respect toward them. When we recognize the daily miracles that God performs for us, our thankfulness is a sign of humility.

1. Make a list of people who have done something kind or beneficial for you. Include at least two family members.

2. For each person on your list, write at least two ways they have impacted your life.

3. Write a plan for gratitude visits, when you will meet the people on your list and tell them what they mean to you.

4. Seek out opportunities to thank God for beauty, goodness, and happiness in your life, and record them daily in a *hakarat hatov* journal.

5. Our tradition commands us to recite one hundred blessings every day. Develop a plan to learn and recite a new blessing every day for a week.

CHAPTER 2

Sh'lom Bayit

One Shabbat evening, a woman stayed late in the synagogue to hear Rabbi Meir teach a lesson. When the lesson ended, she went home, but to her surprise, she realized it was so late that the Shabbat light had gone out. Her husband asked brusquely, "Where have you been?"

"Studying with Rabbi Meir," she replied.

A jealous man by nature, he refused to believe her. "You're not to return to this house until you spit in Rabbi Meir's face," he said. Distraught, the woman set out for the synagogue to pray for guidance. In the meantime, Rabbi Meir heard what had happened, and he went immediately to the synagogue. When the woman entered the building, the rabbi approached her with a pained look on his face. "Do you know a charm to heal a sore eye?"

"Yes," replied the woman, and she spit in his face.

"Now," said the rabbi, "go and tell your husband that you have spit in my face. See how great is the power of peace."

(Deuteronomy Rabbah 5:15)

Family Harmony

Family life is messy sometimes, and no family is immune from arguments and hurt feelings. Fortunately, Judaism acknowledges this fact; for example, the Torah not only depicts human frailties—like jealousy and dishonesty—but also attributes these weaknesses to the spiritual giants of our tradition. When we read that Abraham, Isaac, Jacob, Sarah, Rebecca, Rachel, and Leah struggled with many of the same problems that plague our families, we feel less shamed by our troubles and more confident that שְׁלוֹם בַּיִת (sh'lom bayit, family harmony) can be created.

Building family harmony, however, requires effort. Clear communication, resiliency, a sense of humor, and an awareness of family history are tools that strengthen family life.

GOD TELLS A WHITE LIE

Disguised as guests, three angels visited Abraham after his circumcision. They told him that within a year, Sarah would have a child. Sarah, who was ninety years old, overheard the divine promise and laughed, wondering to herself, "Now that I am withered, **and my husband so old?**"

God heard Sarah's laugh and asked Abraham, "Why did Sarah laugh, saying, "Will I, in truth, have a child, **as old as I am?**" (Genesis 18:12–13)

Notice that God shaded the truth. Sarah doubted the prophecy because she thought Abraham was too old to be a father. God wished to avoid hurting Abraham's feelings and reported to him that Sarah laughed because she thought she herself was too old to be a mother.

According to Jewish tradition, preserving family harmony is important enough that even God misrepresented the truth to maintain peace between husband and wife.

ACTIVITY 1

 RT @King Solomon: **By wisdom a house is built, and by understanding it is established.** #Proverbs #shlom bayit

Open communication is important to family relationships, and active listening is essential to good communication. When we listen actively, we suspend judgment and try to understand the other person's experience and point of view. There are six principles to active listening:
Encourage, Clarify, Restate, Reflect, Summarize, and Validate

Place a check mark in the box that best describes your active listening habits.

	Always	Sometimes	Never
1. I encourage family members to share experiences and feelings.			
2. I ask questions to clarify what the other person has said.			
3. I repeat in my own words what the other person has said.			
4. I use my own words to reflect what I think the other person is feeling.			
5. I summarize the ideas and feelings that I hear from the other person.			
6. I validate (show appreciation for) the other person's effort to talk to me.			

How Do You Face the Heat?

Take this quiz and find out.

Your mother and father disagree about the best place to go for vacation. You:

◆ Tell them that wherever you go will be more fun if everyone is getting along.

◆ Download some information on both places and print it out for your parents.

◆ Stay out of it. It's not your problem, and joining the disagreement will only make it worse.

You are annoyed your parents want you to move out of your bedroom when Grandma visits during Pesach. You:

◆ Ask Grandma how she likes all the cool stuff in your room and mention that you could use some time in there alone each day.

◆ Don't mention it to anyone and try to enjoy your time together.

◆ Call another family member in town and ask for advice.

Your father and older brother are extremely competitive on the basketball court and frequently fight on the court. You:

◆ Let them know that getting along is more important than finding out who's got the better three-point shot.

◆ Talk to your coach about how to soften on-the-court conflicts.

◆ Avoid going to the gym with them.

Your sister begged for a dog, but you're the only one who ever walks him or plays with him. You:

◆ Mention to her that if the two of you could share the load, you would be a lot happier.

◆ Realize that the dog and you are quite content and leave it at that.

◆ Ask the dog walkers in the neighborhood how their families share the task.

Mostly green
Avoid the heat
Like Jonah, the prophet, you steer clear of difficult situations that seem too hot to handle. Instead of telling the wicked people of Nineveh to repent as God had commanded, Jonah "rose up to flee to Tarshish" *(Jonah 1:3)*. In the end, however, Jonah was persuaded to do God's bidding.

Mostly red
Dig right in
Like King David, you boldly confront potentially hot situations, with hopes of finding a peaceful solution. For example, King David sent ten men into the wilderness with instructions to peacefully approach Nabal, an evil adversary, saying, "Peace be to you, and peace be to your house, and peace be to all that you have" *(I Samuel 25:6).*

Mostly blue
Get another opinion
Like Rehoboam—King Solomon's son—you seek outside advice when you face fiery situations. For example, when the assembly of Israel beseeched King Rehoboam to lower taxes, he asked the elders, "How do you advise that I should answer this people?" *(I Kings 12:6)*, though sadly, Rehoboam ignored their good counsel.

Sh'lom Bayit

Judah's emotional plea (Genesis 44:18-34) melted Joseph's heart and enabled the reconciliation (settlement) between Jacob's sons, which is the only "happy ending" for siblings in Genesis. All the others, Cain and Abel, Isaac and Ishmael, and Jacob and Esau, end disastrously. Joseph and Judah demonstrate that sh'lom bayit *can be achieved when families take emotional risks.*

Then Judah **went up to him** and said, "Please, my lord, let Your servant appeal to my lord, and do not be impatient with your servant, You who are the equal of Pharaoh. [19] My lord asked his servants, 'Have you a **father** or another brother?' [20] We told my lord, 'We have an old father, and there is a child of his old age, the youngest; **his full brother is dead, so that he alone is left of his mother, and his father dotes on him.'** [21] Then you said to your servants, 'Bring him down to me, that I may set eyes on him.' [22] We said to my lord, 'The boy cannot leave his father; if he were to leave him, his father would die.' [23] But you said to your servants, 'Unless your youngest brother comes down with you, do not let me see your faces.' [24] When we came back to Your servant my father, we reported my lord's words to him.

[25] "Later our father said, 'Go back and procure some food for us.' [26] We answered, 'We cannot go down; only if our youngest brother is with us can we go down, for we may not show our faces to the man unless our youngest brother is with us.' [27] **Your servant my father said to us, 'As you know, my wife bore me two sons. [28] But one is gone from me, and I said: Alas, he was torn by a beast! And I have not seen him since. [29] If you take this one from me, too, and he meets with disaster, you will send my white head down to Sheol in sorrow.'**

[30] "Now, if I come to your servant my father and the boy is not with us — since his own life is so bound up with his — [31] when he sees that the boy is not with us, he will die, and your servants will send the white head of your servant our father down to Sheol in grief. [32] Now your servant has pledged himself for the boy to my father, saying, 'If I do not bring him back to you, I shall stand guilty before my father forever.' [33] Therefore, please let your servant remain as a slave to my lord instead of the boy, and let the boy go back with his brothers. [34] **For how can I go back to my father unless the boy is with me? Let me not be witness to the woe that would overtake my father!"**

CONCEPT MAP

Judah draws near and in doing so, he takes some risks, which are necessary for intimacy. Without that risk of intimacy, of emotional closeness, the brothers will not be able to reconcile. He especially risks emotional harm, both by exposing his deep love for Benjamin, and by exposing his deep concern for the suffering of his father Jacob.
HOW DO YOU DRAW NEAR TO YOUR FAMILY?

How many times does the word "father" appear in Judah's plea? Why?

Joseph's saga began when his brothers' jealous hatred prompted them to sell him into slavery. In fact, it was Judah who suggested they sell Joseph to the Ishamaelites (Genesis 37:26-27). Now, years later, while pleading to save Benjamin from prison, Judah has finally accepted that his father favors Benjamin (and Joseph), sons of Rachel, who he loved dearly.
CAN YOU RECALL AN INSTANCE WHEN YOU SWALLOWED HARD AND ACCEPTED A PAINFUL FAMILY REALITY?

Some people speculate that Judah fabricated this exchange and that Jacob would not have said this to his own sons. What do you think? Why would Judah have added it to his plea?

Judah's empathy (the state of being sensitive to the feelings, thoughts, and experiences of another) for his father played an important part in the brothers' reconciliation. Read the rest of the story in Genesis, chapter 55. Does Joseph demonstrate empathy toward his brothers?
HOW CAN EMPATHY BUILD SH'LOM BAYIT IN YOUR HOUSE?

AGADDIC TRADITION

The following tale is based on a classic midrash told about Rabbi Yisrael Meir Kagan, known as the Chofetz Chaim.

Once, the **Chofetz Chaim** spent erev Shabbat with friends, who had two children named Jacob and Sarah. The youngsters set the table with the family's finest plates, sterling silverware, elegant candles, sweet wine, and a golden challah.

As the honored guest, the Chofetz Chaim raised the Kiddush cup and everyone sang, *"Baruch atah Adonai, Eloheinu Melech ha'olam, borei pri hagafen!"* The father then reached for the challah and discovered that it had not been covered.

"Oh no! Where's the challah cover?" he exclaimed in surprise.

Jacob's face flashed with anger. "Sarah, you idiot!" he yelled at his little sister. "Why didn't you put the challah cover on the challah? I told you to get it!"

Sarah looked at her brother, then at her parents, and finally at the stunned rabbi. Without warning, she burst into tears and fled from the room.

After a long silence, the rabbi spoke. "You know Jacob, one of the reasons we cover the challah before we bless the wine on Friday night is to spare the challah's feelings. We don't want it to be embarrassed that the wine is being blessed before the bread. If we cover the bread before we say Kiddush, the challah won't see it happening and won't feel ashamed."

He paused and then continued, "If Judaism tells us to worry about the feelings of the challah, how much more should we be concerned about the feelings of our own family!"

ACTIVITY 2

1. Humor can often defuse an angry outburst and preserve family harmony. Instead of crying out "Oh no!" what lighthearted comment might the parents have said when they realized the challah wasn't covered? _____

_____

2. The ability to bounce back after an upsetting (or traumatic) incident is called resiliency. Resilient families cope better with stress, manage meaningful relationships, and enrich each other's lives. Can you suggest behaviors that would enable Jacob and Sarah to bounce back after this argument?

_____

3. The Jewish sage Moses Maimonides (1135–1204) wrote: "If siblings won't have compassion for each other, who will have compassion for them?" What can prevent siblings from feeling compassion for each other? Can you recommend a strategy to prevent repeated crises for Jacob and Sarah? _____

_____

SH'LOM BAYIT SUPERSTAR

This is a fictitious account of an encounter between Judy Blume and a critic who thinks several of Blume's books should be censored because they contain inappropriate subject matter for kids. All highlighted quotes are real comments from Ms. Blume that have been excerpted from her website and from interviews.

Judy Blume rose from her chair and walked to the podium. A petite woman with a radiant smile, she immediately captivated the audience. One man with a sneer on his face, however, stood quickly to ask the first question:

"Good evening, Ms. Blume."

"Hi."

"Your novels *Are You There God? It's Me Margaret* and *It's Not the End of the World* address mature themes, such as divorce, human sexuality, and religion. What gives you the right to publish stories like these on topics that only parents should discuss with their children?"

As if she had expected the confrontation, Judy Blume smiled broadly.

"Thank you for raising such an important issue so quickly." The audience laughed uncomfortably.

"It's not a laughing matter," the man said.

"I agree with you sir. In fact, **I write about sensitive subjects, like family strife, love, death, and school because kids write and tell me these are their immediate concerns.**"

"Yes, yes, I know what you write about," the man interrupted, "but these family matters are for parents to discuss with their children."

"**Kids write me and tell me they wish they could talk to their parents about them,**" she explained patiently. "**They wish their parents would acknowledge their feelings and take them seriously....**"

"Say whatever you wish, but I will work hard to censor your books in schools," the man said.

"**Let children read whatever they want and then talk with their parents,**" Blume answered. "**If parents and kids can talk, we won't have as much censorship because we won't have much fear.**"

"**Love, loss,** joy, sadness, inadequacies, rivalries, hope, hopelessness. What do kids want? They want the same things we all want—a loving family, friends, a non-threatening workplace (that's school for kids), a nurturing, safe environment in which to learn. They want to be encouraged, challenged, and appreciated for who they are, recognized for what they might become, and accepted even when they make a mistake. Don't we all? Most of all, they wish they could talk to their parents, and that their parents would really listen (without judging them)."

ACTIVITY 3

Our tradition teaches that "a group of people and a family resemble a heap of stones: if you take one stone out of it, the whole [heap] totters." Write the name of a family member inside each boulder. Add a brief reason why each person is important to your family.

WHAT I THINK

A home filled with respect, humor, sensitivity, and sharing provides a place for us to connect with one another. When we work toward sh'lom bayit, love nourishes every person, and family life remains strong even when confronted by conflict, change, or challenges.

1. Describe an instance when you spoke or acted in a way that upset the *sh'lom bayit* of your family. How could you have prevented it?

_____

_____

_____

2. . Learning about your family history can be fun. Search online for a genealogy chart template that will help you trace your family history. As you research family members, gather stories about each person, record important events that changed lives, and learn about unique family traditions.

_____

_____

_____

3. Make a list of activities your family enjoys together. Add two new items to the list and develop a plan to try them.

_____

_____

_____

4. Pirkei Avot 1:5 teaches, "Let your home be wide open and the needy be members of your household." Organize a family project that brings this lesson to life.

_____

_____

CHAPTER 3

Emet

Throughout his marriage, Rav's wife tormented him. When he asked for beans for dinner, she prepared lentils. When he asked for lentils, she brought him beans. Eventually, their son Hiyya decided to deceive her so that his father's wishes would be honored. When Hiyya knew his father wanted lentils for dinner, he told his mother that Rav wanted beans. When his father wanted beans, he told her lentils were preferred. The deception worked. Soon, Rav told Hiyya that the dinner struggle with his wife had ended. Sheepishly, the boy confessed his trickery. Rav smiled appreciatively but rebuked the boy, saying, "Do not continue to lie, or you will become like those whom the prophet Jeremiah criticized, saying: 'They bend their tongues like bows' [Jeremiah 9:2]."

Truth

Rav's son, Hiyya, faced a difficult dilemma: Should he deceive his mother to ease his father's suffering? The compassionate son decided that an innocent lie in this case would restore family harmony. Under the circumstances, one might think he made the right decision—after all, Judaism allows us to tell white lies to preserve peace. But in this instance, his father objects. Despite benefiting from his son's dishonesty, Rav urges the boy to stop lying because he understands the consequences; namely, that Hiyya's relationship with his mother might be ruined forever.

The architects of Jewish living recognized that lies undermine trust and that without trust, all social relationships crumble. "The world is preserved through three things," taught Rabbi Simon ben Gamliel, "truth, justice, and peace" (Pirkei Avot 1:18).

Moreover, the Torah (Exodus 34:6) explains that אֱמֶת (*emet*, truth) is one of God's attributes. Our primary task in the world is to walk in God's ways, so we too should always embrace the truth.

TRUTH: A FOUNDATION FOR ALL RELATIONSHIPS

Jewish wisdom counsels us "to keep far from a false word" (Exodus 23:7) because lies undermine family harmony, destroy close friendships, and overturn peaceful societies. The destructive consequences of lying are symbolically represented in the Hebrew word for lie (see below). Our sages observed that each letter stands on a single point, without a firm base. On the contrary, the letters in the Hebrew word for truth, אֱמֶת (*emet*), are stable, each with more than one point to stand upon.

The letter ר lacks a left-sided leg; the letter is unbalanced.

The ק descends below the baseline; it is unbalanced and cannot "stand" on its own.

The ש sits unbalanced on the baseline.

truth **23**

ACTIVITY 1

Follow the example provided and fill in each empty box with a *Lie*, a *Why*, and a *Preventive Strategy*. Be as realistic as you can.

 RT @King David **Who may dwell in God's tent? They who live without blame, who do what is right, and who acknowledge the truth in their heart."** #honest to goodness Psalms

People lie for three reasons:

1. To avoid embarrassment
2. To shift blame
3. To make themselves appear more interesting or important than they are

To change this behavior, try these 4 strategies:

1. Use humor to tell the truth.
2. Recognize that humans are not perfect and fess up.
3. Recognize that truth is the right of all people.
4. Ask yourself how you would feel if people constantly lied to you.

LIE	WHY	STRATEGY
I finished second in the 600-yard dash.	To avoid embarrassment and make ourselves look better	Humor: I must have eaten too much turkey last night, because I waddled like one around that course.

What's Your TRUE Flavor?

Take this quiz and find out.

A music critic just called your brother's band "mediocre." You say:

◆ "Hey, any publicity is good. It's a compliment just to get reviewed in that mag."

◆ "That critic is clueless. You guys rocked."

◆ "Maybe it's a sign that you guys should invest in some better amps."

Your best friend bombs an audition and ends up with a two-line part. You:

◆ promise to help him go over his lines next time.

◆ know his performance was weak, but tell him you were captivated.

◆ celebrate that he got a part, since lots of people didn't.

Your friend failed his science exam. Upset, he turns to you, and you:

◆ hide your "A" paper and say you didn't do as well as you'd hoped either.

◆ sympathize, then quickly switch the topic.

◆ tell him you aced it, but offer to study together next time.

Your friend slips, revealing the name of her secret crush. She begs you not to say anything. You respond:

◆ "Oh, please. That's no big secret. Everybody likes him!"

◆ "I sit next to him in math class. I could find out if he likes you…"

◆ "What are you talking about? I didn't hear anything."

Mostly red
Rainbow sherbet
You always offer an encouraging word but won't offer false praise, as it counsels in Exodus 23:7: "Keep far from a false word."

Mostly blue
Soft-serve vanilla
You make peace wherever you go and might even twist the truth for a higher cause. You embrace the Talmud's decision that says, "It is permitted to alter the truth for the sake of peace."

Mostly green
Rocky road
You tell it straight and quickly come up with a plan for action. You live by Zechariah's advice: "These are the things you must do: Speak truth to one another, and render true and perfect justice" *(Zechariah 8:16)*.

AGADDIC TRADITION

As the queen left the throne room, she instinctively caressed her precious necklace. "I've never seen her enjoy a piece of jewelry so much," said her prime minister to a lady-in-waiting.

The next morning, even before she got out of bed, the queen called for her necklace.

After waiting thirty minutes, she became alarmed. "Where is my necklace?" she shouted.

The servants mumbled something and fled the room.

An hour passed before the queen's mother arrived with bad news.

"My dear," she said, "the necklace is missing."

"Wh-a-a-t?" the queen stammered.

"Your prized necklace is lost," the older woman said slowly.

Enraged, the queen called the prime minister.

"Announce throughout the realm that anyone who finds and returns my necklace within thirty days will receive a generous reward. However, whoever returns the necklace after thirty days will be suspected of theft and beheaded."

Meanwhile, an honest Jewish merchant found the necklace. Although he had heard the queen's announcement, he held the necklace until the thirty-first day, when he took it to the palace.

"Didn't you hear the announcement?" the queen demanded.

"Yes," he said.

"Before I call the executioner, tell me, why did you wait to return my property?"

"Because if I had returned the necklace within thirty days," he answered, "everyone would have thought I did so because I feared the consequences. By waiting, I've made it clear that I only fear the God of Israel, who commands us to return lost property."

His faith, and his honesty, surprised her. "Blessed be the God of the Jews," she cried.

ACTIVITY 2

1. How is the commandment to return lost property related to the value of *emet*? _____
_____

2. How does returning lost property build trust in society? _____
_____

3. The commandment to return lost property refers specifically to an enemy's property: "When you encounter your enemy's ox wandering, you must take it back to him" (*Exodus* 23:4). What is the Torah teaching about trust, truth, and peace? _____

26 truth

EMET SUPERSTAR

"That's him…that's Jimmy Bain," said the nine-year-old, pointing to a picture in the photo lineup.

"Are you certain?" asked the policeman.

"Uh-huh," said the youngster. He looked around the room, seeking approval from the adults; after all, he had done exactly what they had asked: "Pick out a picture of Jimmy Bain," they told him.

James Bain became the prime suspect in the kidnapping and assault case when the victim's uncle suggested that Bain fit the attacker's description that his nephew had provided. The police added Bain's picture to the photo lineup and then violated proper procedure by asking the boy to pick out Bain's picture.

Although Bain maintained his innocence, the eyewitness identification convinced jurors that the nineteen-year-old defendant was guilty, and he was sentenced to life in prison.

BRINGING TRUTH TO THE COURTROOM

Ten years after Bain's trial, forensic science entered the era of DNA profiling. Suddenly, law enforcement officials were able to sample a suspect's DNA and compare it to DNA gathered at a crime scene. If collected, stored, and tested properly, DNA specimens can ensure that truth and justice are carried out in the courtroom.

Barry Scheck and Peter Neufeld recognized that DNA profiling could exonerate (clear) victims who had been wrongly convicted. In 1992, they established the Innocence Project at Cardozo School of Law at Yeshiva University to pursue the truth in cases where innocent people were jailed because of misidentification, coerced confessions, or improper forensic procedures.

Lawyers for the Innocence Project filed a petition for DNA testing in the Bain case. The petition was approved and proved that Bain had told the truth. After thirty-five years behind bars, James Bain was freed on December 17, 2009.

"We started** the Innocence Project as a clinical program at the law school … because we realized that just as DNA could be used to identify the real assailants, it could be used to exonerate people. We also knew that this would be an amazing tool to revisit old cases where people had been dragged out of the courtroom, screaming, "I'm innocent! I'm innocent! I'm innocent!" (*Barry Scheck*)

The Innocence Project estimates that between 2.3 and 5 percent of prisoners in U.S. jails are innocent.

Emet

Like us, our ancestors wondered if it is ever permitted to tell a lie. The Torah seems clear: "Keep far from a false word" (Exodus 23:7). But sometimes there are circumstances when the truth might be more damaging than a white lie. What does our tradition say about times like these?

If someone asks an extremely personal question about a private matter that might be embarrassing, though in such a circumstance, it is preferable to refrain from answering or explaining that the matter is personal.

It is permitted to deviate from the truth to practice modesty.

"If a rabbinic scholar is asked whether he has studied a particular [text of the Talmud], he may answer, out of modesty, that he has not, even if in fact he has studied it." *(Talmud)*

It is permitted to deviate from the truth to practice humility.

If a rabbinic scholar is asked about the hospitality he received in a certain place, he may lie to save his host from being exploited by dishonest people who might abuse his hospitality and cause him serious financial loss. *(Talmud)*

It is permitted to deviate from the truth to prevent someone else harm.

MAP

"And Sarah laughed to herself, saying, 'Now that I am withered, am I to have [a child], with my husband so old?' Then God said to Abraham, 'Why did Sarah laugh, saying, "Shall I in truth bear a child, old as I am?"'" *(Genesis 18:12–13)*

"It is permitted for a person to deviate from the truth in a matter that threatens the peace." *(Talmud)*

"When Joseph's brothers saw that their father was dead, they said, 'What if Joseph still bears a grudge against us and pays us back for all the wrong that we did him!' So they sent this message to Joseph, 'Before his death, your father left this instruction: "Forgive, I urge you, the offense and guilt of your brothers who treated you so harshly."'" *(Genesis 50:15-17)*

When is it permitted to tell a white lie?

"And God said to Samuel, 'How long will you grieve over Saul, since I have rejected him as king over Israel? Fill your horn with oil and set out; I am sending you to Jesse the Bethlehemite, for I have decided on one of his sons to be king.' Samuel replied, 'How can I go? If Saul hears of it, he will kill me.' God answered, 'Take a heifer with you and say, 'I have come to sacrifice to God.'" *(I Samuel 16:1–2)*

It is permitted for a person to deviate from the truth to maintain common courtesy. *(Talmud)*

"It is a commandment to entertain the bride and bridegroom and to dance before them singing, 'A beautiful and graceful bride,' even if the bride is not really beautiful." *(Code of Jewish Law)*

ACTIVITY 3

· ·

Our tradition often uses metaphor, simile, and personification to describe truth. For example:

Metaphor: comparing two dissimilar things as though one is actually the other, as in "The truth is light to the eyes, lying a snare to the feet" (Solomon ibn Gabirol).

Simile: comparing two dissimilar things using "like" or "as." For instance, "The truth is like a tree of life, and from it you will eat all your days" (Sefer Hachinuch).

Personification: giving human qualities to a non-human, as in "The truth is naked and people are virtuous, so they will shut their eyes lest they see it" (Proverbs).

Create your own definition of truth using metaphors, simile, and personification.

METAPHOR

_____

_____

_____

_____

SIMILE

_____

_____

_____

PERSONIFICATION

_____

_____

_____

_____

WHAT I THINK

"Truth is fidelity [faithfulness] to one's word, keeping promises, saying with the lips what one says in one's heart, bearing witness to what one has seen." *(Peter Ochs)*

1. What is exaggeration, and how is it related to *emet*?

2. Telling on someone (tattletale) is a form of honesty. Why is it frowned upon? When should you tell on someone?

3. Psychologists say that every human being lies. One research study claims that people lie (to varying degrees) 25 times a day. What situations tempt you to lie? What strategies can you use to avoid lying when you encounter each situation?

4. Yohanan Tverski, a Hebrew writer, said, "A half truth is a whole lie." Do you agree? Give an example when Tverski is correct? When he's wrong?

CHAPTER 4
Kedushah

A **king intentionally** dropped a priceless gem and then gave a clue to his children as to its whereabouts. He was testing them, hoping they would use their determination and intelligence to find it. Likewise, God has dropped sparks of holiness on the world. Through the Torah, God gives Israel clues regarding the places they have fallen, so that Israel may return them to God. *(Ba'al Shem Tov)*

Holiness

The idea of קְדוּשָׁה (*kedushah*, holiness) is central to Jewish living; after all, God commands us to be holy, saying, "You shall be holy, for I, your God, am holy" *(Leviticus 19:2)*. To be a Jew, therefore, is to be someone who strives for holiness.

Some religions teach that holiness is best pursued by living a spiritual life in seclusion. Judaism disagrees. The task for Jews, explains the Torah, is to bring holiness into the world through our actions: "You shall not steal; you shall not deal deceitfully or falsely with one another" *(Leviticus 19:11)*. Another way to pursue holiness, and thereby enrich our lives, is to transform the commonplace into holy acts; for example, when we recite a blessing before and after we eat or when we wake up each morning or even when we use the bathroom, we elevate those ordinary experiences to a higher purpose.

AIDS TO HOLINESS

The sages who crafted the Jewish way of life developed several aids to help us pursue holiness. The most obvious is the Jewish calendar, which provides many opportunities for us to shift our attention from daily pursuits and concentrate on spiritual rejuvenation. No less important are ritual objects, such as *mezuzot*, *kippot*, and *tefilin*, which remind us of our responsibility to pursue holiness.

GOD-PRISMS IN THE WORLD

. . . .

God-prism is an unusual and imaginative term that explains an important religious idea. In the same way that a prism refracts ordinary white light, revealing the hidden reality of all the colors of the visible spectrum, so too, when we observe God's commandments, our behavior reveals the hidden sparks of God's holiness in the world.

 RT @Rabbi Heschel "The meaning of our life lies in perfecting the universe. We must gather, redeem, and elevate the sparks of holiness scattered throughout the darkness of the world. #holinesseverywhere

ACTIVITY 1

Redeem the behaviors below by placing their numbers in the proper holiness circle. Remember, some of the activities will fit in more than one circle. Place those numbers in the intersection(s) of the appropriate circles.

1. A delicate new moon rests beautifully in the sky as you recite the Kiddush for the New Year.

2. You gaze in awe at the gigantic waves pounding the beach.

3. From the mountain peak you can see one hundred miles across the lush forest floor.

4. You drive to the countryside to get cornstalks to add to the top of your sukkah.

5. You act as a pallbearer at the cemetery during your grandfather's funeral.

6. You interrupt your bike trip to recite the evening service before it gets too dark.

7. You visit your grandmother in the nursing home every Wednesday evening.

8. You read Torah when your sister becomes a bat mitzvah.

9. You eat the first meal in the sukkah with bees buzzing around your plate.

10. The workweek draws to a hectic close, and you rush home for a delicious Shabbat meal.

11. You're asked to blow the shofar during Rosh Hashanah services.

12. You donate your old clothes to the homeless shelter.

13. You wake up in the morning and recite "Modeh Ani" to thank God once again for the gift of life.

14. To honor your parents' anniversary, you're called to open the ark for the Torah service.

SPACE

TIME

RELATIONSHIPS

Where Do You Find Holiness?

Take this quiz and find out.

On a family camping trip, you wake up early and are in the mood to pray because:

◆ You love the early morning, the time of day when you are the most awake and alert.

◆ The sky is a beautiful color, the birds are chirping, and the trees look magnificent.

◆ You remember how everyone worked together to make dinner last night and how you had fun playing games with your family.

You will be visiting your grandparents the first night of Ḥanukkah. You really can't wait because last year:

◆ Your grandmother told a story about her parents' miraculous escape from Poland during the war.

◆ Your grandfather showed you a bookstand that he made for your father's bar mitzvah and said that this year he would start working on yours.

◆ Ḥanukkah is your favorite holiday and you love spending it with your grandparents.

You went to your cousin Yael's bat mitzvah. You particularly loved her speech because she talked about:

◆ The family and how much she loves being with her cousins and grandparents on Pesaḥ and other holidays.

◆ Shabbat and how she appreciates having a day to rest and get away from the stress of the week.

◆ The synagogue and how she feels so peaceful whenever she comes to the sanctuary.

You spent a Shabbat with the family of a friend from summer camp. You were most inspired at Shabbat dinner by:

◆ The way everything looked special in the house—the polished silver, beautiful china, and sparkling glasses.

◆ The way the host family did things together at the table, like singing and telling stories.

◆ The feeling that came over the house at sunset as the spirit of Shabbat entered.

Mostly blue
People person
You find holiness among people who raise your spirit. As the Torah says, "You shall be holy people to Me" (*Exodus* 22:30).

Mostly green
Time trackin'
You experience holiness through time—holy days and special events. As the prophet Nehemiah said, "For the day is holy to God" (*Nehemiah 8:10*).

Mostly red
A place for Everything
You find holiness in places that have special meaning to you. As tradition says, "Remove your sandals from your feet, for the place where you stand is holy" (*Exodus 3:5*).

AGADDIC TRADITION

We cultivate holiness in our lives when we extend ourselves to others; when we stretch ourselves to meet the needs of others, as this legend teaches in a creative way:

When Abraham encountered King Melchizedek *(Genesis 14:18)*, who was Noah's son Shem, Abraham asked him, "Through what deed did you merit survival in the ark during the flood?" Melchizedek replied, 'Through the deed of charity and loving-kindness." Abraham was surprised by the answer, and asked, "How so? Were there beggars aboard that you could perform deeds of charity?"

Melchizedek laughed and replied, "No, but we were preoccupied constantly with the care and feeding of countless species of birds, beasts, and other animals, each requiring very special attention, and this we did day and night with no sleep."

Said Abraham, "If loving-kindness toward birds and beasts can save the world, how much more so can loving-kindness practiced toward other human beings, who are created in the image of God."

ACTIVITY 2

1. The significance of this tale rests on the idea that God rewards humans for adopting certain behaviors. What is Noah and his sons' reward in this legend? How would you recast the reward so that the story is relevant to modern times?

_____

_____

2. Explain Abraham's logic when he says, "If loving-kindness toward birds and beasts can save the world, how much more so can loving-kindness practiced toward other human beings. ..." _____

_____

3. In this legend, performing acts of loving-kindness spreads holiness in the world. What else can you do to spread holiness? _____

_____

4. God commanded Moses to speak to the entire community, saying, "You shall be holy, for I, your God, am holy" *(Leviticus 19:2)*. What is the significance of telling everyone in the community that they must be holy? _____

_____

KEDUSHAH SUPERSTAR

The young woman stared in disbelief at the doctor, probing his face with her dark, penetrating eyes. "Leave Kibbutz Degania and the Kinneret?" she mumbled, speaking more to herself than to him. "I can't."

"Rachel, there's no choice. Tuberculosis is highly contagious, and if you stay and continue your work, you'll infect the children."

As he spoke, the tragedy of her fate overwhelmed him. "Here stands a woman," he thought, "once filled with happiness and fulfillment from rebuilding our Holy Land. Her goodness led her to return briefly to the land of her birth, to Russia, where she cared tenderly for Jewish children displaced by the war. There, she contracted a deadly disease. How could such kindness be the seed of her suffering?"

Even before that agonizing question had fully crystallized in his mind, the doctor knew that there was no answer. But as he looked at Rachel, he sensed that she would spend the rest of her life giving voice to an answer.

Born in Russia, Rachel Bluwstein immigrated to Israel in 1909 and immediately fell in love with the land. Through her poetry, Rachel shared with thousands a glimpse of the beauty of Israel.

"**O**n the Sabbath I used to set out for a rest in the nearby hills. So many twisting crevices, so many dear hiding places, so many green river beds: if only I could remain here all my life. It is good to walk down the path around the shore, until one sees the wall of the city and its round towers. Tiberias is ancient. It doesn't look like a city to me, but rather a drawing in a schoolbook about the distant past. Look, these stones saw the pale face of the preacher of Nazareth. Heard the oral law of the rabbinical sages. And these gray stones even remember the face of beautiful Veronica.

The Kinneret is not simply a landscape, not just a part of nature; the fate of a people is contained in its name. Our past peeks out of it to watch us with thousands of eyes; with thousands of mouths it communicates with our hearts."

(Excerpted from "On the Shores of the Kinneret – The Sea of Galilee – 1919)

Holiness

HOLINESS IN TIME

What are your family's favorite sacred moments? How does facing sacred moments with loved ones enrich the experience?

The goal of Jewish living is "not to amass a wealth of information, but to face sacred moments."
(Rabbi Abraham Joshua Heschel)

"And God blessed the seventh day and declared it holy, because on it God ceased from all the work of creation that God had done."
(Genesis 2:3)

"With love, You gave us holidays for our happiness, You gave us festivals and seasons to rejoice ... and it was the holidays sanctified by You with happiness and rejoicing that You bequeathed to us. You are blessed, God, who sanctifies Israel and the seasons."
(Kiddush for festivals)

HOLINESS IN RELATIONSHIPS

The highest form of human behavior is the voluntary performance of deeds of holiness, which complete God's creation. By teaching us the *mitzvot*, the Torah defines a culture of holiness and guides us in the task.

"God spoke to Moses, saying, 'Speak to the whole Israelite community and say to them: You shall be holy, for I, your God, am holy.'" *(Leviticus 19:2)*

CONCEPT MAP

HOLINESS IN SPACE

Where do you most feel holiness?

Our closest and most intimate relationships are with our family. What specific ways can we bring holiness into our family?

"In our synagogues and houses of study, we can encounter God. But God does not need sacred space. If God is everywhere, then all space is equally sacred, presenting equally an insight into God's presence and promise. Sacred space is religion's accommodation to human beings. Our ... need to witness the special signs of sanctity (the Torah scroll, the Tallit, or the Shabbat candles), to hear the sounds that recall religious fervor (the shofar call or the chant of Kol Nidre) all contribute to our sense of meaning and connection." *(Rabbi Brad Artson)*

"One who deals responsibly and truthfully with others and with whom the souls of others are at ease, it is as if they have fulfilled the entire Torah."
(Midrash on Exodus 15:26)

"When God saw that Moses had turned aside to look [at the burning bush], God called to him out of the bush: ... 'Do not come closer. Remove your sandals from your feet, for the place on which you stand is holy ground.'"
(Exodus 3:4-5)

"God spoke to Moses, saying, '... Let them make me a sanctuary that I may dwell among them.'" *(Exodus 25:8)*

ACTIVITY 3

Make an accounting of the ways you invest in spreading holiness in the world. An example is given for each investment type.

HOLINESS INVESTMENT LEDGER

Investment Type	Investment Description	Purchase Date	Current Asset Value	Unrecognized Gain
Holiness in Time	Light Shabbat candles	Weekly	Rest and rejuvenation	I am more creative
Holiness in Space	I visited Israel with my family	Summer vacation	Fun sightseeing/hiking	Connect with my history
Holiness in Relationships	Help my friends study for test	Every Thursday night	I improve by helping	My friends appreciate me

WHAT I THINK

"We can set aside certain objects for a sacred purpose or celebrate the holy days on our calendar. We can seek out the sacred places in our lives and make them holy or simply act as a channel through which God's work is done in the world, especially in our relationships with others." *(Rabbi Kerry Olitzky)*

1. What are some stumbling blocks that prevent you from becoming a *klei kodesh*, a vessel for holiness in your family? What can you do to avoid the obstacles to holiness?

2. Reciting blessings transforms the commonplace to something sacred. Choose 5 blessings to say regularly for one month. Describe how the practice makes you feel.

3. List seven holy spaces you regularly enjoy. Visit each place during the next month and write a blog about how each space makes you feel. Share your thoughts with your family.

4. Jewish ritual practices, such as lighting Shabbat candles, kissing the mezuzah on doors, and wearing a *kippah*, are designed to bring us closer to the divine. Discuss with your family a new ritual practice to observe.

CONCLUSION

In Family Connections, which is the second volume in the Living Jewish Values series, we have explored four Jewish values that strengthen family relations:

Hakarat Hatov – Gratitude
Sh'lom Bayit – Family Harmony
Emet – Truth
Kedushah – Holiness

In Volume 1, Be Your Best Self, we investigated four values that foster personal growth:

Kavod Habriyot – Individual Dignity
T'shuvah – Returning to Your Best Self
Sameach B'chelko – Personal Satisfaction
Anavah – Humility

Use the Lotus Diagram on the next page to summarize each value you studied. There are eight comment boxes for each value. You may use any of the following suggestions, or list your own ideas about the values, and your reactions to them.

1. What is the Hebrew word for the value?
2. How would you define the value?
3. What makes this value important?
4. How will this value affect your life?
5. What is a strategy you will use to adopt this value?
6. How will this value affect your community?
7. What core text associated with this value most inspires you?
8. How would you prioritize this value in relation to the others you studied?

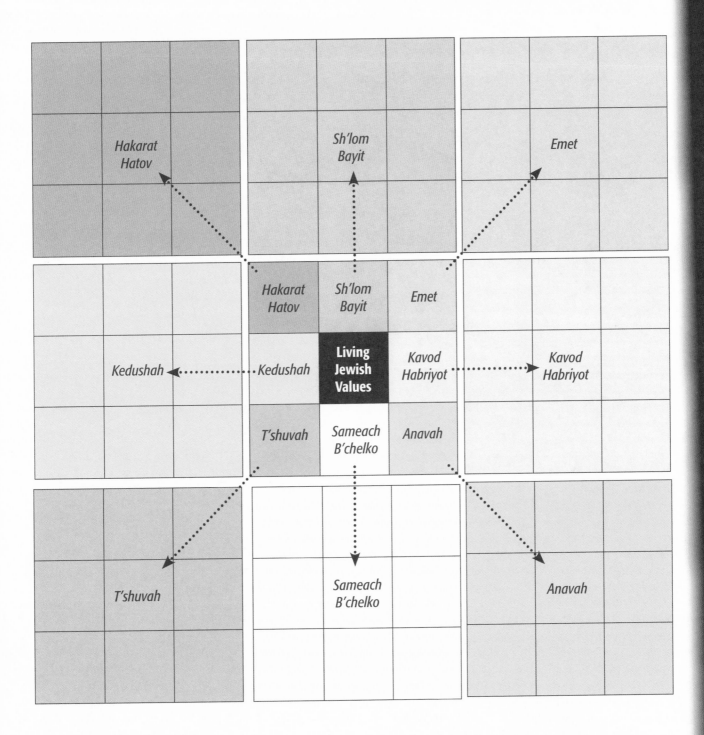